Less Adversarial Cultures

By

Ray Cunnington

ISBN 13:978-1530994410

Copyright Ray Cunnington

First published 2016

Cover illustration: Detail from "The True Issue, or 'That's What's the Matter'" political cartoon, 1864, HSP *Cartoons and Caricatures Collection (3133),* Historical Society of Pennsylvania.

Printed by CreateSpace.

Available from Amazon, Bookstores, and other on line retailers.

Dedicated to

United Nations Manifesto 2000
And members of the Peace Think Tank
Hamilton, Ontario, Canada.

… Towards Less Adversarial Cultures

INTRODUCTION

This is a layman's account of human development from a Humanist perspective. In broad brushstrokes it paints a picture of humankind's likely origins, its efforts to understand itself, and why we face today's dilemmas. It is brief, simple, and shows the way many issues fit together.

The modern world is greatly affected by the past. The manner in which most nations run their countries hasn't changed much since antiquity. Backed by powerful cultures, the governing bodies, law courts, and established institutions continue to be based on adversarial models designed for opposition rather than good management. Leaders and committee members are often selected because of political connections rather than personal merit. There is much antagonism and violence in the systems we have inherited.

In the face of today's world problems, it shows how individuals can make the difference between destructive choices and a more rational future.

CONTENTS:

Introduction...5

Contents...6

1. In the Grip of Culture...7

2. How did we get here?...15

3. The Power of Cultures...23

4. *Time to Think*...29

5. Some Early Developments...30

6. Laws and Penalties...41

7. Ascendance of Money...49

8. Growth of Media...60

9. *Feedback opportunity*...67

10. Old Cultures are hard to Change...68

11. Seeing Things Differently...75

12. *Your Reflections*...87

A Word of Gratitude...88

Appendix 1. UN Manifesto 2000...91

Appendix 2. Links to world resources...92

1.
In the Grip of Cultures

Play fighting comes naturally to young children, but the wars of men are mostly determined by ever-changing cultural beliefs. The thoughts that follow come from observations over a long lifetime.

Cultures have a way of dictating what people think, what they do, and even aspects of their personality; hence the cultures in which they are brought up generally exert a strong influence on how they behave.

Cultures, as I am using the word, are common patterns of thinking and acting that are shared by a particular group. For example, academic cultures expect students to study; football clubs permit kicking and cheering – acts that would be unthinkable in a church or court of law. By understanding common cultures the behaviour of others becomes somewhat more predictable. Those within a culture may occasionally feel confined, but knowing the way to behave provides many with a comforting sense of belonging or acceptance, so much so that the act of being excluded can be extremely painful. But every culture, no matter how inclusive, has limits. Unwritten rules govern what people are allowed to do and what they are cautioned to avoid. Such restrictions are usually maintained quite forcefully by some group members.

Long ago, as a youngster at a boy's boarding school in England, I found myself forced to conform to a culture that was at odds with my own sense of justice because it included a good deal of bullying and violence. Even as a child I wondered why corporal punishment was considered the correct and necessary path to manhood. I did not think it fair that grown men should hit young boys, nor could I understand why nations inflict so much unnecessary suffering on each other, especially in war.

Back in the 1930s, before the Second World War, this traditional masculine culture held me captive, restricting my ability to oppose it. However, when national conscription was approaching, I felt forced to make a stand. By age nineteen I already knew I was determined *not to kill,* so instead of waiting to be enlisted and given a gun, I managed to evade my country's call to violence by volunteering to serve as a medical orderly with the Royal Air Force. This step has affected my life, jolting me to search for better ways to handle conflict and understand how cultures gradually change.

Five hundred years ago many people believed the earth was flat, although a few had shown otherwise. Then Columbus ventured outside his medieval culture and discovered America. This caused no end of mental re-adjustment.

When Galileo demonstrated that the sun did not revolve around the earth, he contradicted the church's teachings and was condemned as a heretic.

Before great new ideas can be widely accepted, millions of people have to change their ideas about how the world works. And that takes effort.

Letting go of old notions is a struggle, often accompanied by anxiety and confusion sometimes leading to acts of violence. Changing familiar ways of thinking are generally vigorously opposed. Since the past continues to exert its pressure on the present. it is easy to understand the slow progress and limited acceptance of controversial concepts such as global warming.

Cultures tend to be amazingly resistant to change. Among the ones most firmly opposed are those that concern religion, family and national duty. Many are based on powerful tales from the past that relate to morals or ways of behaving. Ancient stories don't need to be true to be widely accepted, particularly when they are taught to children very early in life. Although most cultures were created long before any of us were born, religious concepts, myths and fairy tales continue to exert their influence on human actions partly because they somehow "ring true" to personal experience and continue to be endlessly repeated.

Many stories that occur in at least three world religions come from Jewish texts. Here is God's blessing to mankind as translated in the King James Version of the Bible.

> "Be fruitful, and multiply, and replenish the earth, and subdue it: and have dominion over the fish of the sea, and over the fowl of the air, and over every living thing that moveth upon the earth. (Genesis I – 28).

This may have been sound advice given the society of the time but can it still be considered divine wisdom many centuries later when the planet is overcrowded with people and thousands of creatures are becoming extinct? Populations everywhere are waking up to new thoughts about what humans are doing to the earth and to each other. People are slowly recognizing that common actions, once assumed to be "right", may threaten our global future. The past keeps forcing us back into archaic ways of thinking

Towards Less Adversarial Cultures............11

Over the course of human history, civilizations have been far from prudent. Much of their story has been about conflict, betrayal and cruelty. Humans are complex characters with bright and dark sides; they are both Dr. Jekyl *and* Mr. Hyde. And each individual reacts differently to the lives of the folk around them. When dealing with common disasters such as floods and earthquakes they often work together well, but many empires have collapsed because of internal conflict and the gradual depletion of the land and resources upon which their cultures depended.

One bothersome characteristic, especially among rulers, is arrogance or hubris, a know-it-all attitude that refuses to admit to error. Although it is a common problem, it is particularly evident in males. Over the millennia, proud and obstinate leaders have caused much pain for their subjects because of inflexible ideas they inherited from the past. For example, King Charles I of England (1600 to 1649) believed so completely in the doctrine called the Divine Right of Kings that he could never admit he could make a mistake. When he quarreled with parliament his refusal to admit to error provoked a civil war and finally his execution. Many men exhibit similar obstinacy but are unable to see the blindness in themselves.

Rather than change their ways, imperial leaders have relied too much on following traditional beliefs and practices. Some societies have shortsightedly cut down their forests, burned the wood, and allowed too much soil to be eroded, then waged war on others to remedy their deficiencies.

Once upon a time the world was empty of humans; the seas were full of fish and the land was populated with many kinds of life. Gradually the world has been filling up with people and now the seas are warming, the land and air are polluted, and many creatures are facing extinction. The predatory human species has followed biblical advice. It has not only gone out and multiplied, but finally gained mastery over most of the other creatures, usurped their habitat, and come face to face with its greatest challenge: taming the aggressive side of its nature to prevent its own annihilation.

In earlier times, in an empty world, when bands were small and land was plentiful there was always somewhere for families and tribes to move to. Today it is no longer so easy, as populations continue to expand. Everywhere human life is being challenged by lack of water, desertification, war, nuclear dangers, rising sea levels, and unstable climate conditions caused primarily by the excessive burning of fossil fuels in recent times.

Although human achievements have been transformative, human bodies do not appear much different from the days when Paleolithic artists painted their first pictures in a cave. Humanity has virtually the same needs today as it had in the beginning: water, food, shelter and companionship. It also needs a purpose, something meaningful to do.

Since human needs cannot be eliminated, many believe that looming shortages must necessarily lead to violence and war. It seems extremely hard for people to recognize that if humans poison the earth, or compete too ferociously, they will perish along with their loved ones and many other creatures. Are we doomed to destroy ourselves and our world, or can we change the ways we think?

The real bottom line is to find alternatives to the adversarial patterns that cause social friction, inability to work together and senseless destruction. Since climate change is already upon us, the prime question is how intense will cultural conflicts be? How much depletion of the earth's bounty will occur before human greed is satisfied? Will nations fight to the last fish, the last tree, the last piece of earth, or can common global problems become the *starting point of learning to share and care for what remains*?

14. Towards Less Adversarial Cultures

We can begin by reconsidering the creation story.

2.
How Did We Get Here?

Every great culture has its own creation story. And they all have considerable appeal. But if modern research is correct, life originated in the sea, gradually colonizing the land with plants and small animals. Scientists continue to debate whether this miraculous life force was always present, or whether it came from space. But more and more people all over the world are coming to accept that our human ancestors are probably descended from small tree-dwelling creatures that lived mostly in dense forests. After millions of years, distant cousins from these beginnings were diverging into several types of apes.

While all animals depend on plants for food, some eat other animals. In their struggle for existence the plant eaters protected themselves by growing big, by living in groups, acquiring sensitivity to danger, and by fleetness of movement. Their survival strategy was avoiding risk.

By contrast, the carnivores needed to develop combat skills. The path to becoming a successful predator required considerable intelligence. Meat eaters had to develop enough brainpower to outwit their prey while avoiding being killed by others. Young mammals gained knowledge by staying with their parents long enough to learn their skills

In the area where humans were first identified, currently called South Africa, the climate entered a more variable period. This provided an opportunity for some highly adaptable humanoids to take advantage of their competitors. No longer confined to the treetops, they walked upright, allowing them more freedom to travel on open land and use sticks and stones for defence or attack. However, like all living beings, they had to compete for food with other species: large cats, reptiles, wolves, bears, and elephants.

To defend against being eaten by predators, these early humans developed strong cooperative bonds that helped their small bands survive. Their omnivorous diet allowed them to eat a wide variety of foods.

Like other meat eaters, early humans probably possessed built-in reflexes that helped to restrain them from biting or killing their own kindred. Nevertheless, quarrels and minor fights were doubtless common. Like us they were dominated by the great emotions of fear, anger, jealousy and sexual desire. These passions are so overwhelming they can cause sudden surges of energy that some-

Towards Less Adversarial Cultures 17

times become violent. However, in the far distant past they may have conferred an evolutionary benefit, allowing the strong to breed and the weak to die.

Gradually, over another million years or so, some of these pre-human creatures were adapting in new ways. With their growing intelligence and ability to cooperate they were developing a new sense of social order. They were growing apart from much of nature by their ability to put the group's safety ahead of individual wishes. As time passed they learned how to adopt and handle fire. By attaching meanings to verbal sounds they made communication between themselves much easier. But their languages had no conformity; each tribe, each region, developed its own tongue. Within each tribal culture they could begin to converse intelligibly, but understanding other groups was limited.

By this time the men had become formidable hunters who spent much effort crafting the tools and methods that would enable them to kill large animals. Slowly these bands of newcomers were becoming so successful that a few groups started to spread out in search of greater opportunities. So began the 100,000 year migration that would slowly scatter these beings to every part of the earth.

No matter where we live now, it seems all humans come from Africa; all are related by common ancestors, and most of the genes that govern our physiology are shared with our primate cousins: bonobos and chimpanzees. Much human behaviour is squarely based on this primate ancestry; there is a fascinating inner ape in everyone, and it certainly is not evil as some people suggest. In fact *it is the foundation on which human civilization has been built.* Our species is a miracle of the life force which is still evolving new abilities.

While it is impossible to know what our ancient relatives were really like, we can perhaps imagine them with a temperament similar to ourselves. Simply to survive they needed a powerful sense of loyalty and caring. They probably liked tricks and jokes and understood ideas of give and take. But like us they were often irritable, anxious, gossiping, grumbling, and arguing, sometimes getting hot with anger. Even their feelings of vengeance were perhaps the first signs of an immature form of justice. In short they were strong, inventive, affectionate, mischievous, cruel, clever, and totally absorbed in the doings of their particular culture, for which many would sacrifice their lives.

These early ancestors were naturally curious about the great forces that sometimes overwhelmed them: rainstorms, thunder, fire and flood. They wanted to know who or what possessed the awesome powers that affected them so acutely. A heightened sense of *self-consciousness* was dawning; they were becoming aware of their own mortality. They needed answers to the troubling questions of birth, death, and a possible afterlife. Could it be that the spirits of the earth were angry with them? Were their dead ancestors still alive but unseen? Did the deceased continue to hold grudges, or cry out for revenge? In the absence of better knowledge they made up plausible answers.

In their huts and meeting places shamans and charismatic leaders mesmerized the population with imaginative stories, doubtless in much the same way as parents sometimes mesmerize their children. The elders told terrifying tales of ancient times when mythic heroes vanquished fearful demons. The deeds of these godlike figures were believed to have brought great benefits to their tribes. Special thanks were always accorded to the immortal figures that were victorious in fights, saving them from dreadful fates. Such stories helped to keep the people united, provided warnings for their children, and kept their spirits up.

And who could dispute the truth of events that happened in the time of the ancestors?

For thousands of years, throughout nearly all of human existence, humans have been dominated by cultures of superstition and fear. If someone died unexpectedly some kind of magical influence was suspected. Rituals were developed to keep evil forces at bay, to bring rain, or provide more abundant game. Tribes expected their leaders to use secret spells or prayers to assure prosperity, and certain places deemed sacred were set aside where ancestors could be worshipped and relatives safely buried. Sacrifices were seen as essential, either to gain favour with the gods, or to avoid their anger. Special food was laid out for the spirits to share.

Almost all cultures and languages were filled with potent words that referred to mystical creatures with supernatural powers, such as talking animals, giants, spirits and demons, sorcerers, ghosts, fairies, and witches. Thoughts about magic and religion are buried deep in folk traditions the world over. Because they have such a long human history many such beliefs are still potent and continue to be seen in literature and art today. Ancient signs still exert their magic, not only in temples, mosques and sacred buildings but also as symbols of national or political identity. Since each religion upholds a somewhat different idea of truth, individuals continue to argue over ways to worship and which is the real God. Others question whether God even exists.

This is the point where science and religion diverge. As with many disputes, the same phenomena can be seen from various viewpoints. Since conflicting beliefs continue, it is easy to understand the plight of our ancestors as they quarreled and fought over each other's views and customs. It is easy to believe that a particular God intervenes in human affairs like a divine parent, and most people can probably think of examples. But whether one believes the universe is governed by God, or by some kind of magic, a more pertinent question is whether the gods or supernatural forces are influenced by human actions? Do they *care* what any of us do? Do prayers work? Are sacrifices effective? Are the symbols men die for any more substantial than illusions?

How do we know the real cause of what we call "acts of God"? Are they divine interventions, examples of magic, or the random effect of humans acting upon themselves? Do religions give us support, or do they divide us by providing elements of conflict? We still don't know for certain but, before the advent of experimental science, sacred opinions held sway for millennia and could not be effectively disputed or challenged.

3.
The Power of Cultures

To appreciate the strength of magic, mystical and religious ideas, we must return to the influence of cultures; for it is deep within the family that most of these long lasting concepts first take shape. Children are complete human beings long before anyone starts to call them black or white, Muslim or Hindu. It is adults who impose these designations upon children, labels under which each child must live.

Families can be likened to social laboratories in which anxious babies first learn to respond to the warmth and soothing of their caretakers. This is where a child's earliest brain patterns are laid down. These highly sensitive creatures are exposed to many kinds of influences as they attempt to understand their world. Carl Jung described the situation more than a century ago in his book The Theory of Psychoanalysis: "In the little world of childhood with its familiar surroundings is a model of the greater world." The child looks up to its parents for guidance and protection in much the same way that populations look up to their leaders.

Children are born the most wonderful, up-to-date models of a human being that can possibly be. These newcomers have already received their genetic programming and can signal what they like and what they don't like. Protecting these precious beings from harm is why children need so much love and attention. For, although they are resilient, they will not remain unaffected by the cuts and bruises they will face as they enter the adult world.

Small children watch and listen to everything going on around them; they study the words and facial expressions of their parents, their siblings and others close to them, looking for meanings and good ideas. They are natural plagiarists, copying, cutting and pasting other peoples' thoughts and ideas into their own brains. But they do not always copy them exactly, or understand them correctly. They cannot tell which messages are true or false. If they feel happy they will show their delight; if not, they may throw themselves into the tantrums and emotional displays that often cause so much family conflict and misunderstandings.

Infancy is the time when children first start to talk and when they may be introduced to a particular set of beliefs. Generally they are unaware of being socialized. When all goes well, the warm feelings that develop are just the beginning of a mutual sense of love and security that keep families bonded together.

Healthy youngsters have boundless faith that the world is made for their pleasure; they take kindness for granted and are seriously put out if checked or thwarted. But children must learn to control their impulses, their hunger, their tempers and their sexuality; they must not be permitted to run riot, bite or punch others. Absolute freedom must be curtailed for a mutually satisfying society to exist. Here is where love and compassionate training make such a difference; for each child begins life unaware of human values and may not accept cultural interventions easily. In most cases the same people who provide loving homes must also impart discipline.

During these early years, the miraculous life-force gives parents an almost hypnotic influence over those in their care. Those who preside over this period inevitably provide lasting models of the culture they represent, both positive and negative. For many parents this means teaching obedience and a sense of duty.

Wherever love and fairness are developed, most children attempt to conform. But when trust is eroded, child-rearing is likely to take a more adversarial path, for it is during this early upbringing that a child's concepts of right and wrong are being formed.

In the family home the child watches how its caretakers treat each other and how they deal with conflict. Toddlers learn quickly how they are expected to respond. Are family stories to be hushed up? Or are they free to be talked about? Are conflicts met with anger and violence or as temporary matters to be resolved?

When a youngster has particular difficulty learning to talk or read, some adults think the child is *bad*, or not trying hard enough to cooperate. If children spill milk, or refuse to eat with a spoon, there are some people who believe they will pay more attention if hit or spanked. Much that we call evil starts when adults get so angry they are unable to control themselves and mistakenly use punishment to "teach their charges a lesson" instead of helping children to understand the true situation.

Since every child develops strong feelings about its caretakers, a battle of wills can become the start of a child's ambiguous behaviours towards those who look after them. For some unfortunate youngsters, home is where they may first experience bad behaviours such as lying, bullying or ill-treatment. They may discover that racism and sexism are so deeply ingrained in some adults that they assume bigotry and sexism are "normal". Many learn to copy bullying behaviours; how to hurt or annoy others. Such spiteful attitudes are generally picked up earlier than more positive teachings, such as fairness and negotiation.

In a few cases children can be so dominated by the influence of their peers, relatives or other dominant persons, they may feel excessive need to act out their fear, guilt or shame. They can feel compelled to follow ways they do not wish, leading to self-harm, addictions or other obsessive-compulsive disorders. At the other extreme of parenting, some youngsters are so overindulged they never receive adequate guidance about where to draw the line or set reasonable limits on their actions.

During the brain's growth almost all children go through a period of make-believe or false cognition, sometimes called "magical thinking". This is a time when some parents may think their child is telling lies. But this may be an inaccurate interpretation. Many fanciful fears or wishes may appear to the child-mind as true, or something they would like to be true. Children often believe they have special powers as they interact with the fairy-tale world of Santa Claus, friendly animals, monsters, dragons, and witches. Generally, as they grow older and listen to new stories, these magical ideas tend to fade. But traces of early beliefs and ways of coping may secretly continue into later life, especially in the case of superstitions and religious matters.

Long after childhood events or persons have left the scene, an inner "phantom family" continues to influence much non-conscious thinking. Positive memories are generally absorbed without difficulty, while frightening or hateful ones can stay suppressed or denied for a lifetime.

There is a disturbing link between cruelty in the family and violence in society; for it is the socialization of the early years that make cultures so durable. But while upbringing exerts its influence, each individual's brain is his or her own creation. Developing an independent, mature mind is a life work; far harder than growing an adult body.

4.
Time to Think

Before starting the next section you may find it useful to give yourself a short break. You may want to reflect about what you found true. Perhaps you will recall examples from your own family and how you and your parents resolved conflicts. Give yourself a few moments and write your thoughts here:

_____

_____

_____

_____

_____

_____

_____

_____

_____

_____

_____

5.
Some Early Developments

This section and the next three provide a few examples of the ingenious ways in which our ancestors tried to improve their lives while struggling to maintain order in changing times.

Humans are opportunistic, always seeking growth and advantage but, although their early efforts were well intentioned, they often adopted self-serving customs that led to conflict between themselves and their neighbours.

Ten thousand years ago, in fertile places, an important shift was taking place in human development. A few tribes were giving up hunting as a primary way of living and were starting to husband their animals instead. Perhaps because game was becoming scarcer, other small groups were settling down in fertile valleys and planting land. A more reliable source of food was becoming possible. Agriculture was beginning to develop, and a few innovative folk were turning their hands to building settlements. While each family maintained its own individuality and social practices, new ideas were being voiced about relationships and the possession of goods and territory.

Since only women were endowed with the miraculous power to give birth, females had always been revered for their grace and wisdom. Wood and clay images of women were among the oldest artifacts produced, and children often traced their lineage through their mothers. However a growing familiarity with farming and husbandry may have upset an earlier balance of the genders. The practice of planting seeds may have allowed some males to claim that the coming of children didn't depend on mothers, but upon the all-important seeds that men planted into females. Worse still, some men even argued that children no longer belonged to the women who bore them, but to their fathers instead. Slowly the sacred goddesses that had been worshipped for millennia were losing devotees while male gods were becoming more dominant. Patriarchy was starting its ascendancy.

If this suggestion is even partially true, one cannot help but wonder about the psychological changes it must have made to intimate relationships. Men broke the maternal bond with children and treated women as property, sometimes not much better than cattle. Child marriage was commonly enforced.

When food was plentiful, populations expanded. But the food supply was always precarious; bad weather or outbreaks of disease could spoil the harvest. Too many mouths to feed could spell starvation. Some unfortunate tribes whose numbers had grown beyond their ability to feed them were obliged to take drastic action to limit further growth and get rid of unwanted babies. Some thought it necessary to make human sacrifices or leave newborns to die by exposure. Such gruesome acts, the ghosts of which still haunt us, were probably not deliberate cruelty, but pragmatic survival efforts.

From time to time local feuds must have upset the general tranquility of the countryside as the goals of one group interfered with those of another. Cattle must have been stolen, and conflicts doubtless erupted between the herding tribes who required large ranges to feed their stock and the farming tribes who wanted to keep animals away from their tended plots. To stop people from upsetting the neighbourhood, local rules and understandings about property were probably applied with considerable force. However, in spite of all the difficulties, herding and agriculture were producing far more food than hunting wild game.

Once modest wealth was achieved, the richer families wanted to know how much they possessed. How many sheep or goats did they own? To keep records, numeric symbols came into being. In some civilizations the mystical signs were gradually transformed into the earliest modes of writing. Those who could understand the symbols gained new powers over those who could not. Writing made words permanent, a factor that enabled some stories to endure far longer than many of the tales passed on orally.

Agriculture was producing wealth, and society was dividing into different classes. Instead of living from hand to mouth, a favoured few were beginning to do well. Ruling cliques, wanting to maintain their power, found they were most secure when they kept their followers busy.

In the lulls between harvests there was often a temporary surplus of labour. These times provided opportunities for improving living conditions. Priests and religious rulers called for sacred tombs and monuments to be erected in honour of gods and kings. Fine new palaces were built in emerging centres. Before long thousands of men were engaged in quarrying and transporting huge blocks of stone over long distances, whether for the pyramids, Stonehenge, or other wonders of the ancient world, sometimes to aggrandize a single individual.

Virtually all the energy needed to build the new civilizations was provided by oxen, horses and human labour. There were no machines to ease the burden. To force unwilling animals to obey their masters physical violence was necessary. Whips and goads prodded reluctant beasts, while much cruelty was inflicted on men, women and children.

Most of the new wealth was created by peasant farmers whose backbreaking work was essential, but whose voice had little effect on how their region was run. Often treated more like domestic animals than humans, their harvests were depleted by tax collectors and petty thieves who doubtless squabbled over the spoils.

With life becoming richer and more complex, the growing prosperity was not to remain undisputed; all this wealth naturally attracted thieves. A few disgruntled sons or envious rulers from nearby lands broke ancient customs of non-aggression by forming raiding parties to loot the harvest and capture women and livestock.

Many people have been taught that war is part of human nature. This has often been stated as a fact. But when populations were small, the organization and control needed for genuine warfare may not have been possible. While fights and small-scale skirmishes must always have existed, humans are quite reluctant to kill each other. Recent archeological discoveries suggest that some early civilizations were prosperous long before warfare as we know it was developed. Games and feats of strength may have satisfied the need of young men for power and dominance. Sacred rituals may have kept rival groups from attacking one another.

However, once the peace of a community had been shattered by violence its people cried out for protection. The ill-treated settlements began to defend themselves by raising walls and fortifications. Men took young boys away from their mothers and trained them to act as sentries and defenders.

But walls were not enough to protect people and property from being overwhelmed. After being vandalized, each looted city felt such violation that its citizens were determined to obtain revenge, no matter how long it took. As one community after another was despoiled, the impoverished inhabitants started to rebuild in more effective ways. Usually their misfortunes united them so strongly that they finally became able to overcome their former conquerors. In this way an escalating series of bloody conflicts began to follow each other in endless acts of retaliation. Gradually, as civilizations rose and fell, conflict after counter-conflict began to engulf the ancient world.

The primary foundation of war becomes clear: *War is directly linked to wealth (and the widespread poverty it leaves in its wake).* The costly preparation and maintenance of big armies only makes economic sense when there is something of outstanding value to steal or defend. The seizure of new lands can be an irresistible temptation. Plundering and enjoying other people's riches is a lure that attracts many willing helpers, especially if the base motive of ill-gotten gains can be replaced with ideas of glory, respect, and praise for the heroism of those who took part.

While theft can be relatively easy for a determined attacker, it is quite another matter to keep possession of the loot. Acts of robbery and their accompanying violence stir up a fury that almost inevitably leads to retribution. Successful raiders therefore found it necessary to conceal the true motives for their conquests by denying their responsibility. Some blamed their victims: "Our foes deserved it," or: "It was ordered by our Gods."

Triumphant leaders generally claimed they had divine approval for their conquests, and winning battles often became the accepted method of demonstrating whose God was the most powerful.

Since land, kindred and property were at risk of being seized by marauders, force was perceived as the natural way to protect society. To save their thrones, kings and princes prepared themselves by building up their armies and developing the arts of war.

Warfare is all about protecting one's own by doing harm to others, particularly to rivals. Military power involves secrecy, stealth and surprise, with little concern for human life or consequences. An enemy must be clearly identified, and battle plans hatched behind closed doors. To stir young blood to action malicious tales about the atrocities committed by one's enemies need to be frequently repeated. Foes should be ridiculed, scorned, and depicted as animals or less than fully human. To prepare for battle, troops must be trained to follow orders without thinking. And to produce the fighting spirit needed to kill other humans, soldiers are taught their duty by a brutal discipline.

The Bible provides plenty of information about ancient warfare and the slaughter of women and children. To make children "good", king Solomon advised fathers to beat their sons.

> 'Chasten thy son while there is hope, and let not thy soul spare for his crying.' (Proverbs Ch. 19, Verse 18.)

When one remembers the power of parents to injure their children, this royal approval of punishment provides a shocking excuse for mistreatment. Down the ages millions of vulnerable boys have been subjected to physical abuse by generations of dutiful parents. Tyranny is not a crime of kings and emperors only; it is a latent potential in each of us. The ancient world did little to reprove cruelty, violence, sexual abuse or slavery; in some cultures these painful ways continue to the present day.

Of course there have always been those who mourned the loss of life in war and struggled against the system; many appeals were made to the gods to bring lasting peace. Sometimes, in place of a pitched battle, an agreement could be made for an outstanding warrior on each side to determine the outcome by single combat. This probably saved the lives of thousands of troops, since in those days even minor wounds could lead to infection and death.

In their search for safety many ancient societies glorified the image of masculinity. Young men not only acquired physical conditioning by perfecting such skills as horsemanship, archery and spear-throwing, but also embodied their tribe's social principles and codes of behaviour. Becoming a warrior was a sign of manhood, whether or not actual fighting took place. However as wealth and the number of warriors started to increase, the risk of conflict intensified between rival groups as war began exacting its price far and wide.

In many parts of the globe, in China and Japan, for example, as well as in some smaller communities, states began to see each other as enemies. In the Middle East and the empires of Greece and Rome, war became endemic, with cruelty to children especially frequent in cities such as Sparta that were particularly warlike.

The details of courage and battle, told so dramatically in the Homeric ballads, for instance, lay a good deal of onus on the immortal gods for men's suffering. They claimed it was not men's fault if the gods bewitched them and caused them so many problems. By painting themselves as the tragic sport of capricious immortals, ancient storytellers justified their group's violence. Warfare was glorified. Descriptions of battles immortalized their fighting men, giving them an aura of greatness. Boasts about the courage of their soldiers and exaggerations of their triumphs allowed every male to imagine himself a hero. The Armed Warrior became the supreme patriarchal image of masculinity, with pillage and rape widely recognized as normal rewards for conquest. Clearly the *culture of war* was fully developed many generations before the modern world was born. Stirred by primeval feelings, many people continue to be fascinated by similar tales of excitement and bloodshed on television and film today.

6.
Laws and Penalties

It can be disputed whether *history* is written by those victorious in war, but it is clear that it is the winners who write the *laws.*

Among the warrior kings who fought for dominance in Mesopotamia some 3,700 years ago, King Hammurabi of Babylon stands out. In his attempt to give his rule legitimacy he made a sizeable contribution to social order when he compiled the first known set of written laws.

By combining earlier documents his scribes spelled out what acts were forbidden and the penalties exacted for breaking the rules. Persons in conflict were not allowed to settle disputes among themselves. By taking vengeance out of the hands of ordinary individuals and imposing known consequences upon those who committed crimes, the king discovered he brought more order to the community and greatly increased his authority.

His type of law was based on the painful principle of retaliation or retributive justice: an eye for an eye, a hand for a hand. But all punishments were not applied equally. The lightest penalties were reserved for full citizens; more severe ones were inflicted on commoners, with the harshest ones imposed on slaves. By modern standards the punishments were extreme: "--his eyes shall be torn out -- his limbs shall be broken -- he shall receive sixty lashes with a rhinoceros whip." Death, mutilation and fines were some of the brutal penalties imposed. In those days such acts would not have been considered evil by those who were highly placed. It was not uncommon for the mighty to enforce their authority through fear and pain including flogging, branding, the cutting off of ears or hands, imprisonment, torture, and death. Such acts appeared to be justified when done by those in power, and doubtless a few others not so highly placed sometimes copied their example. Of course this was a far cry from Justice which, in theory, should protect the weak from the strong.

In spite of the callous indifference to pain and suffering, a clear set of laws helped to make life more predictable. No matter how much the people grumbled, the rules determined the outcome of many quarrels, clarified how the different classes should be treated, and encouraged trade. Hammurabi's laws were so useful to the running of a state that kings and governments have continued to impose strikingly similar codes to this day. While most societies do not currently cut off people's hands, the nature of the penalties still depend upon whatever a ruler's court decrees.

Since punishments are designed to hurt, the widespread use of deliberate pain on a global scale must contribute significantly to human suffering. However the ideas that those in authority are unfair, that the rich may be treated quite differently from the poor, or that the heavy hand of justice may cause unnecessary harm, are rarely questioned. The public takes it for granted that punishment deters evil-doers. There is much denial that the present system is biased or could possibly be improved.

Lawbreakers are said to be "brought to justice". But does inflicting punishment really succeed in making things "right"? Does it reduce crime and provide opportunities for restitution or rehabilitation? A big problem is the way the *fear of punishment often suppresses truth*: people in tight corners frequently tell lies.

In the courtroom, those charged with crimes often expect lawyers to "tell a good story" or make legal excuses to "get them off." Many who are found guilty spend more energy on denying their wrongdoing than in accepting the truth they are responsible for their antisocial acts. The adversarial nature of the law itself can sometimes prevent evidence from being heard and truths from being known.

Because of secrecy and cover-ups many high-level crimes go unreported. Innocent citizens may be afraid to speak, and guilty ones find safety by saying nothing. To avoid being shamed or punished, the great majority will cover up, minimize, or attempt to blame others. Because so many resort to falsehood the author and psychologist M. Scott Peck calls our society "People of the Lie."

According to Statistics Canada, less than 35 percent of crime is reported to the police and less than five percent result in convictions. If such a large percentage of the crimes are not reported or never come to court, one has to wonder whether this retributive system is adequate for the problem. Does it motivate the bulk of society to do right, or is most of its capacity spent on deterrence that may not deter?

Some citizens feel a perverse thrill when engaged in rebellious acts. Street crimes and gang activity are prime examples of their disregard for the law. Rivalry and wounded pride drive some to get *even.*

A few damaged souls discover they *enjoy causing pain.* Isolated individuals who nurse grievances can believe committing murder is necessary to appease their anger or demonstrate their potency. The frequent shootings in American schools and colleges appear to be examples of their rage (or perhaps their desperation).

Even the massive war on drugs has done little to reduce the demand for contraband. However the extraordinary money that can be made from trafficking has greatly increased the violence associated with it, much as Prohibition did in the 1920s.

Of all the casualties of punishment, perhaps the most injured are those who learned to punish themselves. These tortured souls see themselves as wicked. By internalizing their pain they may engage in self-destructive behaviours, becoming addicted to drugs or lives of self-loathing. Some wind up in hospitals, in psychiatric wards, or in prisons; some mutilate themselves; others commit suicide.

The law claims its punishments keep our communities safe by sentencing "bad apples" to prison for lengthy periods at the public expense. But while most offenders will eventually be allowed back into society, few will return unscathed. The bulk of inmates in North America are not given much help to overcome their criminal thinking before being released; hence there is a high probability that more than a few will offend again.

Unfortunately punishment is *highly addictive to those who wield authority;* it tends to encourage the punishers, while doing little to change the criminal behaviours. For a short time those at the top may enjoy an intoxicating feeling of power over others, but this does not last. All too soon the offending conduct starts again and may have to be put down many times.

The common response to disobedience is to make the punishment more severe. If a smack on the wrist doesn't produce the right result there are always those who advocate something more serious. Some cry "get tough on crime" and call for a return to the death penalty. But even death may seem too small a price to satisfy some people's craving for retribution. Over the centuries every kind of torture and humiliation has been tried by those in power without achieving compliance. For if the truth be told, deterrence is not in the hands of the punisher. The human spirit can transcend both fear and pain. Whether fully sane or not, those who refuse to obey their tormentors may choose death or martyrdom. Such people are called saints or heroes by some, while others call them freedom fighters or terrorists.

At pivotal times quite ordinary people can change the course of history. Everywhere there is a limit to what people will stand without rebellion, and when large numbers join together to obtain more freedom there can be revolution or civil war. It is to avoid such sudden changes in circumstances that governments rely on force to protect the powerful few from the masses of the weak.

Of course many people are afraid to rock the boat or challenge the state's power. Not too many stand up for the poor, the vulnerable, those who have lost their homes, or been injured by the state. Even well-meaning people do not want to hear too much about the plight of others. Most go along with the crowd, believing their willingness to look the other way is a sign of their peaceful nature. Few want to admit that sometimes, like some of their leaders, they may be guilty of taking unfair advantage of those less fortunate than themselves.

The adversarial basis of our modern law has changed little since antiquity. It has not only grown old, but parts have become somewhat fossilized. Our laws are a system designed to punish, not to heal or rehabilitate. Unlike evidence-based medicine, the law draws its strength from historical precedent rather than scientific principles. Little research is done on whether or not some longstanding legal assumptions are correct and whether they address the circumstances of humanity's complex nature.

The law justifies the state's violent forms of retribution, but does little to teach people how to handle disagreements constructively, or with a minimum of pain. Very little help is provided to restore shattered lives or achieve more positive outcomes.

If future generations want greater justice from their laws it would be good if the system could become less adversarial. Justice is not a battle between the defence and prosecution, but a last attempt to find solutions to serious problems. The ill effects of punishment need to be re-examined and all forms of torture outlawed, including long periods in isolation for convicts, and the hitting of children by parents. If the goal of corrections is to restore tranquility and promote reconciliation, the law could make greater use of mediation and listening to the quiet voices, especially those of women and children. Where applicable it could institute court-supervised healing sessions where victims are safe to speak truthfully face to face with those who injured them.

7.

Ascendance of Money

With wars rewarding the most aggressive leaders, and laws safeguarding their share of the profits, the next step for those with wealth was the growth of commerce.

Long before money was invented, agriculture was producing a surplus that could be shared. In earlier times this generally took the form of gifts or barter. Gifting is reciprocal, creating powerful bonds between people who feel obliged to pay back what has been freely given.

By contrast, buying and selling are adversarial activities: the buyer's goal is to pay as little as possible; the seller's to extract the maximum price. However, since people needed goods, bargaining became a common practice.

Initially there were no standard weights or units to confirm the fairness of a transaction. To repay favours or to provide a dowry, tokens such as cattle, pottery, or coloured feathers were sometimes accepted as payment. In some areas, cowry shells or pieces of metal were commonly used as a currency to purchase goods. While taxes were generally paid in kind, some rulers began to develop rudimentary forms of money that had standard values. This convenience saved time and effort, especially when trying to purchase the fine goods being offered by traders who had travelled great distances by boat or caravan.

By Roman times copper, silver and gold coins had come into use and were being routinely minted. In addition to their value in trade, coins marked with a ruler's name or likeness provided convincing evidence of the monarch's influence, for it was largely the leader's power that supported the money's value. In major cities, people were beginning to switch from simple barter to a system that ran at least partially on coinage.

Because of its scarcity and special properties, gold was particularly prized by the affluent. To protect their precious metal from thieves, some enterprising goldsmiths started to provide vaults and strong rooms where the rich could store their gold for a fee. Not content with this benefit, the goldsmiths found they could increase their income by lending some of the stored gold that didn't belong to them to new customers. Naturally they charged a fee for the service; hence a system of lending with interest came into being.

Borrowing money became a common practice especially among impoverished members of the ruling classes. But fees were high. Borrowers not only had to pay back loans within a stated time, but were also obliged to pay interest at whatever price the lenders chose to ask. If the fees were particularly onerous it was considered usury and much debate centered on whether it was ethical. After the Roman Empire converted to Christianity, a succession of popes ruled that loaning money was to be interest-free among Christians. As time went on, although usury was still forbidden, some Christians started to get around the ban on interest by exchanging letters of credit. Before long, amassing wealth was considered by many as a sign of divine approval.

With the discovery of the New World in the late 15th century, the search for gold propelled the conquistadors to travel to the ends of the earth to bring back riches for their kings and to adorn their places of worship. Papal Doctrines of Discovery allowed explorers extraordinary freedom to bring the wealth of "savages" to Europe. In some of these newly discovered lands the white traders often mistook the generosity of the natives for simplicity. They found that aboriginals were often willing to provide exotic furs and other goods in exchange for a few boxes of glass beads or trinkets. Once the traders showed off the advantages of their firearms, the sale of weapons became a particularly profitable enterprise that brought European warfare and methods of fighting to the rest of the world.

Since affluence was a way to enjoy almost all the advantages of nobility without its obligations, many goldsmiths branched out into "banking", offering to store other people's valuables safely, in addition to money lending. Under experienced supervision, banks could amass big profits by lending other people's money to customers at sizeable rates of interest. However, loans always carried the risk that some borrowers would not repay their debts.

Initially each banker supplied his own letters of credit, as did many towns and governments. However, as some of the credit notes proved to be almost worthless, banks required a clearing house where the value of such investments could be better determined. Stock markets grew up that provided broad opportunities for anyone with spare money to gain additional capital.

The great attraction of the stock market was the lure of gaining money without having to work for it. By choosing wisely from a variety of offerings, investors had an opportunity to increase their gains, transforming a small stake into a tidy sum. But while prices could go up they could also go down. As investors studied their profits, it soon became apparent that markets behaved in unpredictable ways. Certain commodities could continue rising reliably and then suddenly fall, like the South Sea bubble which collapsed in 1720, leaving many investors bankrupt. It was as if an invisible hand was rocking the financial boat. Although this free hand fluctuated, a free market was considered a necessity to test an investment's value.

In spite of risks, banks were quite willing to put idle money to work by lending loans to wealthy industrialists and government agents to invest in stock. Since every loan was required to be repaid with interest, an ever-increasing spiral of indebtedness could be generated. Capitalism is a brilliant way to make some people rich, but it was never designed for the poor; still less as an international distribution system. Transactions don't have to be fair; price does not guarantee value, and cost may be arbitrarily inflated.

While good investments may bless some with fortunes, the influence of wealth can degenerate into an ongoing process of the rich taking money away from the poor. Money can cause the subjugation of countries. During the 17th and 18th centuries the constant wars in Europe and the tussle for colonies prompted intrepid bankers to change the fate of nations by making massive loans to the right customers.

Among imperial ventures, the colonization of India stands out. Rather than a straightforward military conquest, this was a slow takeover of a country's wealth by a few merchant adventurers who backed their deals with military force and administrative rule. By using private armies and less-than-fair trading practices, the small British East India Company gained so much power that by the 1770s the whole Indian subcontinent was becoming enslaved, unable to defend itself. With so much to be gained, the value of money continued its ascent, eclipsing the suffering of those whose lives were devastated by the process.

The adversarial aspects of trade are clear: capitalism has always used wealth for its own ends. Patriotism provides a justification for a nation's lucrative trade in arms. Everyone wants to have the best, most effective and largest number of weapons. Behind the pressure of international competition there is a big war machine. Free trade isn't truly free; it is generally coerced through deceptive trading practices and military might. The whips and violence, which once played such a major role in keeping workers at their toils, have gradually been transformed into overwhelming fears of debt, unemployment, shortages of food, or becoming a failed state. Deprived of control over their own assets, many urbanized societies can no longer feed themselves. They must rely on governments and big corporations to provide the necessities.

The international money culture can be seen as one way the rich and powerful continue to seize for themselves the wealth that belongs to humanity in common. In the early industrial age, for example, rich families enclosed much common land for their own benefit, land that had previously been available for all. Thousands of peasants were turned out of their homes to make way for sheep grazing, or forced to move into ramshackle towns to work in the new factories. Others were shipped overseas to distant lands where they could be enlisted to fight against poorly equipped tribes in European colonies. All was justified under the name of progress.

Commercial companies continue to appropriate common resources today. Their constant need to increase trade, to expand the market, and get someone else to pay for what they want, creates needless demand for unnecessary activity. Their ruthless competition has resulted in too much consumption with its bloated attendant wastes. In vast tracts of land where commercial companies once traded in furs, timber and spices, the powerful multinationals must now dig deep into the earth to extract the planet's non-renewable resources of oil, metals and precious minerals. Elsewhere they deprive native communities of their livelihood by damming their rivers, then selling the water back to the ones who can pay. While excessive advertising and promotion may profit a particular country or multinational, it can prove disastrous for humanity as a whole. Supporters of the Occupy Wall Street movement can rightly ask how does one percent of the population gain so much while the 99 percent do not? Today's religion has become "moneytheism" not monotheism.

Predatory banking, backed by great power, is incompatible with genuine democracy. But ideas of fairness were never part of the system. Fairness depends upon who sets the rules. Should non-renewable resources, such as coal and oil, really be classed as *income* rather than as global capital? Should the mass of voluntary work, typically provided by women, be counted for nothing in most financial statements? And for what reason are the costs of cleaning up disasters perversely classed as "healthy commercial activity" in the Gross National Product Index?

As aboriginal prophets have warned for decades, "you can't eat money". Profit should not be put ahead of all other concerns, particularly at a time when climate change can threaten survival through progressive loss of food production. The adversarial rules of commerce are all man-made and could be made to serve society better if there were more agreement about common purposes.

The idea that capitalism will make everyone rich is largely an illusion. The modern world's gain in living standards has mainly come from the increased energy provided by fossil fuels, and the great inventions and discoveries of recent times.

At its best money circulates in the economy in much the same way as blood circulates in the body. Like the red blood cells that deliver oxygen to every part of an organism, a certain amount of money is needed to provide life's essentials. If all goes well and money circulates freely the needed goods can be purchased and delivered in good order. But, as in a living body, there can be malfunctions or illnesses that upset the system: the worst outcome is when the money ceases to flow. A financial collapse is like a heart attack, as when the stock market crashed in 1929. When transactions are blocked or go slow, it is like arteriosclerosis. Unfortunately there is no emergency heart or pump to ensure the red cells reach all parts reliably. While increased demand will automatically stimulate the flow of funds, no such advantage goes to where the need is greatest. Those who are poor have no access to unearned interest.

Of course, as is true for most things, money itself is neither good nor bad: it is the use to which it is put that causes problems, in this case the extreme disparity of wealth. When poverty is widespread, its deprivations take the form of mass violence. There is something grossly wrong with laws that insist that the poorest people must always repay the richest lenders when it may not have been the poor themselves, but their rulers, that borrowed the money that put them in debt in the first place.

In spite of its shortcomings, the wealth produced by trade has transformed society. An impressive degree of trust has been built up by the dedication of large commercial companies and their workers. Business leaders and their employees often display great loyalty among themselves; many working long hours and frequently sacrificing family life for the good of their corporations. The culture of finance has its share of heroes and heroines. Money is seen as highly reliable by many of the world's great nations, and a few outstanding philanthropists give their fortunes away.

Nevertheless it would be welcome news if the money system could become less antagonistic and more sensitive to international conditions. Corporation owners could provide more opportunities to those who do the physical work, such as helping workers' cooperatives to flourish. Money could help solve many more problems if the flow could be directed towards reducing want, rather than providing excessive benefits for the fortunate. Instead of rich monopolies, money could provide clean drinking water for developing countries, better education, and the cure for many diseases.

What began as a practical way to provide loans to needy customers has gradually grown into an economic system whose partisan rules threaten human welfare and the health of the planet. The shining prospect of sharing the world's resources is being held back by an adversarial culture whose reliance on military force endangers international stability.

8.
The Growth of Media

The way we look at life depends greatly upon what we are told, and the way matters are explained to us. Since words express the essence of our cultures the introduction of printing in Europe around 1450 gave those who could read and write a great advantage. Instead of books being copied by hand, many duplicates could now be printed at one time and distributed to towns far apart; making the sharing of knowledge more widely available.

This power of the written word soon began to affect all levels of society, even though most people couldn't read. Words possessed almost a religious authority as reading was formerly the domain of the clergy. If something was printed it was generally believed to be true. Printing made information more available as it brought ancient wisdom from other lands to scholars and philosophers, stimulating art and the birth of science.

As the spread of knowledge gathered speed, schools were springing up and there was a growing population able to read and write. Political pamphlets and novels were becoming more common. Individuals were expressing their own opinions without having to find a highly placed patron before their ideas could be printed. By the middle of the 19th century, once steam and electric power became available, printing machines were able to turn out thousands of copies of daily newspapers and bulk books for the mass market.

All this writing and reading had a potent effect on the public. Education was becoming essential; lending libraries were being demanded by working men. Writers and publishers were gaining influence; new voices were heard; unorthodox opinions were introduced in national affairs and many social improvements came about. Influential groups began to consider matters like cruelty to children and animals, and there were rumblings about allowing women to vote. In addition to the flow of comment from the pulpit, the media started to take over the way stories were told, often turning social issues, into heated debates, with the editor assuming the role of judge.

Newspapers boldly suggested who to vote for, what kind of government should be elected, and pontificated on all matters of trade. Print advertising was becoming so lucrative it allowed commercial companies great power to influence editorial content. Since disturbing news and fighting words tended to attract readers, writers exaggerated conflict, often describing elections and political rivalries as if they were fights between gladiators, or jockeys battling for the winning post. News editors generally scoffed at ideas of peace because they thought it unrealistic; besides they knew that nothing attracted readers more than reports about pain and disasters.

Since competition for sales was the life-blood of commercial journalism, truth was often laid aside; sensationalism was taking over at some cost to the facts. Papers sprung up championing nearly every popular opinion. Some supported the government while others upheld the opposition. National identities were artificially built up through a diet of patriotic items and flag-waving, while foreigners were deliberately belittled.

By 1914 printed media had become powerful political institutions that included alternative views on events depending on what readers in Paris, Berlin or London wanted to hear. Commentators from all sides were telling European heads of state they had no option but to go to war. While many people agreed; it was a distortion of the truth. Leaders always have options; it is *the public* that has no option but to obey.

The First World War spurred the development of powerful new inventions that affected how people lived and behaved. The gasoline engine provided more flexible energy than coal and steam, permitting the development of many new inventions such as automobiles and aircraft. Moving picture pioneers started to reveal tantalizing new possibilities: the freedom to travel by motor car, and gripping images of men and women engaged in social upheaval.

Another agent of change was radio broadcasting. Its messages could be understood without having to read, and the medium carried music as well. Radio attracted listeners all over the world, reaching many more people than print. Broadcast voices amplified the effect of Nazi propaganda during the Second World War while also spreading the growth of American influence. Radio and movies were extensively used by both the Nazi and the Allies in their efforts to stir up patriotic support, while vilifying their opponents.

The launching of the atom bomb and the destruction of Hiroshima and Nagasaki in 1945 became a consuming topic for the media. Both the U.S. and the USSR had been allies during the war in spite of long-standing differences, but conflict between them started to intensify almost as soon as the armistice was signed. This rivalry gradually turned into an all-out propaganda battle for people's minds. Capitalism was pitched against communism with stories and spies undermining trust everywhere. Many leaders held the view that the best way to ensure peace was by building up military forces. This logic led to an arms race by both superpowers to build more missiles and nuclear weapons than the other, far exceeding the number required to exterminate the bulk of the world's population.

To prove the superiority of capitalist societies, freedom was presented as the principal benefit of the Western world. In practice this meant freedom to travel, to buy goods, and spend one's money as one pleased. The advantages of consumerism became more clear as the war factories finally began making products for peacetime. Time-saving devices and easy credit accompanied the introduction of television.

The Korean War (1950-53) and the disasters of Vietnam (ended 1973) were the first major conflicts to be seen on TV. With the carnage on the frontline being shown in people's living rooms, some men burned their draft cards and protest songs were aired across the country. But the horrors of the battlefield were far away, and television was so engrossing that many people tried to forget bad news, preferring to hurry home to watch their favourite films or comedy programs.

Later, with the growth of market competition, some media networks found they could gain more viewers by presenting crime news and violence as entertainment. Audiences found the numerous murders and disasters on their screens strangely compelling. Fearful of dangers beyond those they had ever thought of, they were becoming desensitized to the rise in violence that was taking place around them. The role of heavily-armed police, battling it out on the streets with protesters who were throwing rocks, was central to this kind of programming. Films and television have generally continued a trend towards justifying violence.

Big corporations have always been good at spinning exaggerated or misleading stories. The media sometimes amplify small events so greatly that the scandals of a single individual can rock a nation. The Princess Diana stories are a case in point. Today there is real confusion about what to believe. Secretive government departments conceal their manipulations on the grounds of security. Sophisticated public relations experts, with huge vested interests, manage the news. Some of these organizations held back the reality of climate change for many years. Deliberate lies and misinformation is mixed with genuine news, making it hard for conscientious individuals to know how to act. Trivial issues are exaggerated while important matters are ignored or suppressed.

Today, with satellites, the Internet, the smart phone, digital photography and the growth of social media, there are promising new opportunities for direct personal communications to affect the future more positively. Ordinary people's thoughts and pictures are being shared around the world. Citizen journalists are everywhere reporting on matters of interest with the result that the cut and thrust of politics is better understood and many dirty secrets are harder to conceal. Millions of new voices are clamouring to be heard; thousands more stories are available. Never has there been such a torrent of opinion from all parts of the globe. And that offers hope, as well as danger.

Since today's stories will influence tomorrow's world, how can all this communication be used for better understanding between people rather than eroding trust and causing more pain and grief?

Towards Less Adversarial Cultures............67

9.
Feedback Opportunity

There is much to think about in the social changes that have taken place in the last 20 or 30 years. You may wish to take another pause to record your views. Your thoughts and feelings are important.

_____

_____

_____

_____

_____

_____

_____

_____

_____

_____

_____

_____

10.
Old Cultures Are Hard to Change

Humans are good at quarrelling over trivial issues, but they do not normally kill each other. Arguments never cease about how men or women should behave, but their differences don't necessarily lead to violence.

Whether the disagreements concern food, sexual behaviour, how people should dress, the symbols a person should wear, or proper ways to worship, ideas about what is "right" and what is "wrong" are generally shaped by what people were taught as children. Because each culture imposes its own rules and limitations there are wide variations about what individuals are expected to do.

As we have seen, many past civilizations have endorsed violence, kept slaves, amassed wealth, followed unfair laws, and believed inaccurate ideas. Yet few leaders have voiced any guilt or remorse for those they hurt or destroyed.

At the heart of violence there is a paradox. Both the strongest and the weakest want safety for themselves, and believe that organized violence can provide it. The most powerful use it as a means to get what they want, while the weakest often favour violence in the hope that it will control the powerful and protect them.

Although the majority is against bloodshed, it doesn't take much force to compel most people to do bad things. A single person with a gun can do it, just as tanks, drones and missiles can terrorize larger communities.

Most humans are capable of hurting others, especially when ordered to do so. There are always some willing to use lethal force against a vulnerable group they see as enemies.

Though democratically elected governments may be less willing to use violence than dictatorships, the act of casting ballots does not eliminate the possibility of putting someone ruthless in power. It is a very narrow view of freedom to assume that democracy is assured simply by the act of voting every few years.

Inside the high-pressure atmosphere of political wrangling, some of the players can get so engrossed in winning points for themselves or their parties they become blind to the faults in their thinking. It can become too hard for them to see things from alternative points of view, especially if it means forfeiting their positions of power or personal advantage. Vindictiveness and heightened tensions may distort their better judgment. In such situations, costly decisions may be taken and, occasionally, insane orders given: for example, Hitler's Final Solution that launched the Holocaust, or Napoleon's disastrous order to invade Russia.

What made these decisions so catastrophic was that millions of loyal subjects carried out their orders blindly, murdering each other and destroying much of what they held precious because of an over-developed sense of duty to their homeland.

Those in power naturally try to shape politics to suit their times and personal interests. But rather than trying to reduce their reliance on force, some want to increase it. The world's nations now spend some *two trillion dollars* on weapons and their military every year. This massive overproduction of armaments provides some jobs and gives the illusion of safety. But in spite of all the battle fleets, aircraft and missiles, humanity is not protected from harm. The world is not made safer by producing more killing machines. And the funds spent on the military leave less money to cut pollution or improve lives.

Except for the United Nations, there is hardly any mechanism for de-escalating an arms race or reducing conflict. And even the United Nations has difficulty trying to keep peace, partly because the world's *peoples* didn't set the rules and partly because the institution has little means of enforcement. It was founded in 1945 by the five victorious countries that had just fought the Second World War at a cost of some 60 million lives.

Those who attempt to promote peaceful ways, including United Nations committees, are sometimes faced with deliberate roadblocks. All governments do not want peace. Some denounce their peace community as lacking in loyalty and patriotism.

Although the UN has produced some outstanding work on human rights and its call for a Culture of Peace, it is still a league of nation-states, many of whose leaders disagree with each other and are in deep denial about their contributions to violence. Big nations bully smaller ones, and national rivalries are central to the private political games that are sometimes played out. Indeed, the power to make war is probably the last thing some countries will abandon since they have paranoid fears about revolt from their own peoples, and concerns that ill-intentioned rivals are trying to diminish their position and advantages.

Clearly something is askew with global decision-making. Small wars and acts of violence cause millions of people to become refugees with no place to live. Meanwhile the world's bloated militaries maintain their missiles on hair-trigger alerts, ready to destroy the great cities of the globe at a moment's notice – on the orders of a few individuals.

Power and control over others are hard privileges to give up. Those in high places are understandably reluctant to share their benefits. And those lower down don't want to acknowledge their own complicity in seeking gains. These are very human faults, but they are not acceptable excuses. Nobody is wise enough to be trusted with supreme power.

Seen from the perspective of history, most wars and battles do not solve international problems: they *complicate* them. Even small skirmishes can flare up and spread like a malignant cancer.

The two opponents shown struggling on the cover of this book did not intend to pull their world apart and fight the American Civil War. But for all their virtuous intentions their inability to back down led to the slaughter of some 625,000 lives and left deep scars not fully healed 150 years later.

War is a horrific madness that breaks out from time to time between antagonists determined to blame and hurt each other. In the ancient world, no matter how many were killed, such slaughters did not endanger the globe. By contrast, the spectre of modern war on a crowded planet is a different matter entirely. Modern warfare is a wholesale generator of disrupted lives, children orphaned, overflowing refugee camps, hardship, corruption, dislocation and loss. Whether by accident, or design, a major exchange of nuclear warheads exploding on cities, could destroy much of civilization in an afternoon. Emergency medical response would be quickly overwhelmed, leaving parts of the planet at risk of nuclear winter or radiation-poisoning, disasters that few might survive.

Although war is highly contagious, it is *a preventable disease*. There are remedies that could be applied. Like smoking and other afflictions, the addiction to war is curable over time. But first the sickness has to be acknowledged. It cannot be blamed on "bad apples," foreigners, or other people alone. Too much blood has been shed not to seek negotiated settlements. Large-scale hostilities are almost always avoidable if the underlying grievances can be addressed early enough by those willing to negotiate fairly. But that requires a return to sanity. Quarrels need to be addressed at the *talking stage*, while they are still small, before they develop into fighting.

Peace order and good government are the very cornerstones of what ruling bodies are for. At a time when climate change poses one of the greatest challenges to survival, peace is not an idealistic notion of fringe groups. Peace provides an opportunity to set matters to rights; a chance to live life to the full, unburdened by the obligations and wastefulness of warfare. While peace is often discounted, it is not some kind of monotony to be avoided, but a necessary condition to allow time for the errors of the past to be mended.

Since global warming is already causing devastation on many continents and the extinction of many species, there is an overwhelming need to prevent the deliberate destruction of any more land and resources through war. Armies leave a giant ecological footprint because they have little concern for other people's life or property.

If humanity is to have a sustainable future, there is a pressing need to find better ways to handle disagreements than by falling back into fighting. When the powerful can't or won't think about the public's welfare, the people need to fashion a positive role for themselves. It is time to look for some helpful answers, ways intractable conflicts can be transformed to serve more creative goals.

11.
Seeing Things Differently

Nobody likes to be hurt – so how can ordinary people make the future less painful, with less violence and global disasters?

Many who want peace see themselves as good hearted, denying any responsibility for causing pain, holding the view that wars, conflict and violence have nothing to do with them. Many blame outsiders and wish they would stop their aggressive actions. After more consideration, they may begin to admit that murder and violence are not exclusively committed by foreigners but also by their own people, sometimes in their own cities, occasionally by their own families. They may even discover hostile tendencies in themselves.

While it is human to fight for a principle, violence provides no opportunity for finding common ground. One cannot change someone's deepest beliefs through brutality and torture. Changing ideas comes through discussion and agreement. To work out common problems we need to speak truthfully to each other without fear of being criticized or discounted.

At the centre of humanity there is something absolutely wonderful. There is a vital core of goodness that propels people for the sake of those they love to go to work, grow the crops, cook the food, build the houses, nurse the babies, look after the sick, and maintain an ever-ready sense of humour. This is the love that sticks together in times of trouble. In spite of being criticized, ridiculed, and lied to all too often, it knows that life is a precious gift and, when the chips are down, is *willing to give up its portion for the sake of others.* This is the pioneer culture that, by sharing morsels of food and helping each other out, has saved humanity from oblivion countless times.

Rather than seeing power as coming from the top, groups all over the world are beginning to recognize that the real source of power is deep down, that it is *people*, not rulers, who collectively keep cultures going. This is the force more powerful, the ever-present humanity that remains potent below the surface. For it is *ordinary people*, the very ones who have been repeatedly misused, neglected, criticized and put down for millennia, who, in times of trouble, have the inner wisdom, strength and stamina to make changes to the ways we live and to re-energize the human species.

Exceptional figures such as Gandhi, Martin Luther King and Nelson Mandela have followed their own paths to greater understanding. They have demonstrated that *non-violent warriors* can be amazingly successful in helping vulnerable groups stand up against oppression

The promise of non-violence was clearly expressed long ago by George Fox, founder of the Quakers and a passionate Christian. In 1660 he testified before his king that "the Spirit of Christ, which leads us into all Truth, will never move us to fight and war against any man with Outward Weapons, neither for the Kingdom of Christ, nor for the kingdoms of the world."

Modern societies expend much time and money on education. This is an important step in the right direction, but today's programs are often geared towards developing the latest technologies and preparing young people for the demands of the workforce. What often gets squeezed out of the present curriculum is time for deep reflection about what it means to be human and the complexities that involves.

One day, in addition to morals and religious prescriptions, a culture of peace may help us *not* to injure each other. The social costs are far too high for the antisocial acts of individuals or governments to go unchecked. We do not need to destroy each other's homes and achievements simply because our ancestors did. We are perhaps the first creatures on earth with the kind of brains that can learn to override our destructive emotional urgings.

At the present time few people seem to be interested in finding ways we might live together without treating each other badly, or destroying the planet on which we all reside. Even when solutions are finally well understood, it will still take time for people to adjust their thinking and gradually absorb the changed ideas.

While no one can "un-happen" the bad deeds that took place in the past, hurt feelings are hard to get over. Injured people need a great deal of love and consideration. Acts of compassion or solidarity are much more helpful than seeking blame.

Recent findings show that humans can go on learning and changing their ideas right into old age. Grown-ups are not bound to follow the myths they were taught as children. Adults can re-educate themselves; indeed, older brains are far more pliable than was once believed. Wherever people live, individuals can make a positive contribution to their communities. Instead of thinking, "There's nothing anyone can do to make things better", it is more accurate to say, "Each of us has a lot more power than we think."

Changing behaviour is possible, especially when there are teachers and campaigns to support the change. An excellent example is the recent transformation in regard to smoking. Once accepted as normal, the disease-causing effects of smoking are now recognized and societies worldwide have cut back on tobacco use. In similar ways individuals could be made aware of how their unconscious feelings of envy hatred or anger compromise good decisions by destroying friendly human relations. Once this process is more widely accepted, programs could be set up to help both aggressors and victims learn how to lessen vengeful thoughts and give up some of their resentments.

A humanistic "science of peace" would help us recognize the consequences of what we do. One branch would continue along the path of Galileo; pitting the voice of truth against falsehood. Gifted scholars and whistleblowers, brave enough to risk upsetting the powerful, could be given more protection when they prove the words of authority false. Such persons would continue to expose such matters as misleading government statements, accounting fraud, or the way some big companies try to hide the fact that what they are doing may be destructive to the planet and hazardous to human health.

A different branch would follow Columbus in exploring and discovering new realms for human advancement. This field offers much opportunity for research and for providing helpful answers, not only about global survival, but ways to de-escalate conflict as it arises, rather than allowing it to build. How can we develop safer, kinder ways to treat each other? Why must workers go on building so many weapons of war? Why are great states still able to commit crimes without outcry?

At the start of the 21st century, the United Nations used a science-based approach when it adopted Manifesto 2000, proclaiming an International Year for the Culture of Peace. After thousands of years of feuding, here was a call for the entire world to develop less adversarial cultures.

Instead of telling government leaders what to do, the UN spoke to the world's *peoples* directly. Each individual was urged to take responsibility in six areas of their lives by pledging the following: "In my daily life, in my family, my work, my community, my country and my region (I will) Respect all life, Reject Violence, Listen to understand, Preserve the planet, Share with others, and Rediscover solidarity."

Locally, in Hamilton, when this news was first announced, I was among a number of social activists who heard it. Some of us were so impressed with this development that we established a local Culture of Peace network, intending to spread these ideas widely. It was a terrible blow when, a few months later, the twin towers in New York were destroyed and the U.S. military turned its attention to fighting in Afghanistan. Since that time the drumbeat of war has hampered many peace-building efforts.

It is unfortunate that so few people in North America were ever told about the Culture of Peace. However, across the globe, some 75 million individuals accepted its principles and have continued to follow the United Nations ideas. Imagine what giant steps could be taken if more families in every city adopted just one of its six recommendations: "Practice active non-violence, rejecting violence in all its forms physical, sexual, psychological, economical and social, in particular towards the most deprived and vulnerable such as children and adolescents."

In spite of doomsday forecasts, globalization has created a far more cohesive world than ever before; people know a lot more about each other and how to make peace than they did. Over the millennia families have become tribes; villages that were once enemies have formed counties; rival cities have stopped defending themselves with walls; small states have united to become nations; and former foes have joined blocs. Perhaps humans are not as violent as they have been told. Clearly cultures are not immutable; what was once thought impossible can now be overcome.

Everywhere there are millions of individuals and groups trying to change cultural attitudes towards aggression. Artists, educators, and scientists are seeing the world in new ways. Women in particular are busily creating new cultures that are helping them regain their ancient influence. A new spirituality is being born that sees goodness in almost everything except lies, bullying and warfare. Considering that most humans retain a powerful religious faith, it is well to note that virtually every religion teaches peace among its followers. Changing the ancient patterns of intolerance towards each other may come painfully slowly, but much progress towards a fairer world has already been accomplished.

Groups such as the Red Cross, Doctors Without Borders, and hundreds of non-government organizations are changing world ideas of justice and the pressing need to relieve poverty. All these dedicated workers are genuine peacemakers, although they may not think of themselves that way.

Many good people are doing extraordinary things. Mayors for Peace, International Physicians for the Prevention of Nuclear War, and the United Nations are examples. An International Criminal Court has been set up; many nations have banned the use of chemical and biological weapons; there is a landmine treaty in effect, and even abolishing nuclear weapons is being taken seriously by many nations. Never has the world had so much knowledge or power to bring about positive gains.

Beyond the concept of nation states there is the growing idea of *one world*, the promise of cooperation on a global scale. However, unlike the cruel colonial models of the past, this need not be founded on hierarchical principles with a vast army run by a single imperial authority controlling the whole world. Instead it could consist of a series of regional governments that serve the people by keeping peace in their own communities. Where international governance is needed it could be scattered among many cities and countries, as the World Health Organization and the International Civil Aviation Organization are today.

Humans are not good or bad. They are eminently adaptable and most can be educated for a more peaceful future. Even the most aggressive men have a loving side. With fewer stories about abusive conduct in the media, most young men could learn that violence and sexual cruelty are no longer acceptable male behaviours. Positive role models could demonstrate better ways for men to deal with their destructive impulses.

Moving towards a more rational world will take great leadership. And it will require much practice by people. But holding on too tightly to the old adversarial models makes no sense.

Over and above the duties we owe to others, individuals have a duty to themselves and their grandchildren to conserve the future of the world. If we humans are causing climate change, we owe it to those who come after us and the life of all sentient beings to take a stand against the way we continue to pollute the planet. Changing society may feel like an impossible burden, yet for the common good, communities have changed their cultures countless times. Many have changed their gods.

Towards Less Adversarial Cultures

Every positive word you speak and every helpful action you take is a move towards greater harmony. There is much meaningful work to be done. Don't wait to take action. Discuss useful ideas with your friends and relatives.

We all belong to the same species. From a global perspective *there are no outsiders*; there are no heathens or barbarians. Together, in place of racism, we can foster inclusion; in place of sexism we can help establish equality; where there is cruelty we can plant mercy; from a culture of deception we can cultivate honesty. Nowhere is there permission to do harm. Human survival will not be achieved by hurting others and fighting catastrophic wars, but by cooperation.

God or Nature has provided each of us with the incredible gift of choice. Even if we can't always love our neighbours, at least we don't have to hurt them; we can create a better society; *we don't have to fight each other to get our needs met.* We can become more caring, less judgmental. For the sake of our wonderful planet and everything we hold dear, we can refuse to be each other's enemies. Although our choices may differ, while we are alive they are ours to make.

A less violent world is possible.

It is in our hands.

12.
Your Reflections

It is time to reflect on what you have read. Do you agree with peace-building and violence-reduction? If so, please write down your ideas about ways you might contribute towards a less adversarial society.

_____

_____

_____

_____

_____

_____

_____

_____

_____

_____

_____

_____

A Word of Gratitude

My first wish is to give thanks to all the people whose words, thoughts and actions provided the inspiration for this work. It would have been impossible to complete such a task if I hadn't spent much time studying in the company of wise individuals who were willing to share a little of their knowledge about history, peace and human behaviour. For their help and for those who are caring for the planet in other ways I am deeply grateful.

Concerning humanity's desire to be free from war, I can only guess at the wisdom that would result if some university or learned institution were to gather together and share the many peace traditions of the great cultures of China, Japan, India and the Middle East, together with insights from aboriginal communities.

Many times I have attempted to write about the causes of war and human conflict; the first being when I was a young airman stationed at a medical outpost on the banks of Assam's great Brahmaputra river during the Second World War. I wish I could have known more when I was younger but now, as an old man living in Canada, I hope my view of life has become a good deal more inclusive.

Towards Less Adversarial Cultures.........................89

This work's many limitations are mine, together with my restricted knowledge beyond my Western and post-Christian heritage.

Long after I reached an age to retire I had the good fortune to associate with many fine people who had been working for peace most of their lives. By joining the group in Hamilton that was supporting the Manifesto and the UN Culture of Peace I learned much I didn't know.

By pondering the deeper meanings of Manifesto 2000 we all gained more insight about the way individual actions can affect others. Our members seek to resolve differences in peaceful and respectful ways that have taught me patience and helped me to grow in empathy and compassion.

Nearly a whole generation has grown up since the attack on New York in 9/11 yet, in spite of almost constant warring taking place on the international stage, Culture of Peace Hamilton has remained vibrant. With little support and virtually no money it has raised awareness, held meetings, cooperated with other groups, attempted to create safe havens for vulnerable minorities in downtown areas, continues to organize a local peace luncheon twice a year, and has donated and planted hundreds of white narcissus bulbs in the city's peace garden.

From the beginning of history, small groups have been the vehicle for human progress. Individuals gain satisfaction when their members meet together face to face and share their deepest thoughts respectfully.

For me personally I have been additionally blessed by being part of a small sub-group we call the Hamilton Peace Think Tank. While few in numbers, this band of truth-seekers seems to me exceptionally gifted. I have no doubt that useful insights can be discovered by almost any group of concerned individuals who truly listen to each other with open minds.

While everyone may not be focused on peace, everyone has exceptional qualities. When truthful talking and respectful listening is the goal, new wisdom has a chance to emerge. Truth is the springboard to right action, providing a renewed sense of purpose, and the feeling of doing something worthwhile. Whatever your interests, you can take part, or help provide opportunities for such friendly connections.

Ray Cunnington, Hamilton, Ontario, 2016

Appendix One:

United NationsManifesto 2000
drafted by Nobel Prize winners and UNESCO.

Respect All Life: Respect the life and dignity of each human being without discrimination or prejudice.

Reject Violence: Practice active non-violence, rejecting violence in all its forms: physical, sexual, psychological, economical and social, in particular towards the most deprived and vulnerable such as children and adolescents.

Preserve the Planet: Promote consumer behaviour that is responsible and developmental practices that respect all forms of life and preserve the balance of nature on the planet.

Share with Others: Share my time and material resources in a spirit of generosity to put an end to exclusion, injustice and political and economic oppression.

Listen to Understand: Defend freedom of expression and cultural diversity, giving preference always to dialogue and listening without engaging in fanaticism, defamation and the rejection of others.

Rediscover Solidarity: Contribute to the development of my community, with the full participation of women and respect for democratic principles, in order to create together new forms of solidarity.

Appendix 2.

Links to Some World Resources

There are many groups and organizations around the world engaged in fostering ecology, peace and non-violence. Many are local or have local branches you could join.

The major faith and religious groups also have their organizations for protecting the earth and peace and violence reduction.

In addition to groups, a whole new range of books are available about climate change and peace and social justice.

An on-line search in any of these areas will quickly reward your enquiry.

A few direct links to peace groups may be of interest to present readers.

In Hamilton:
www.cultureofpeacehamilton.com/
www.humanities.mcmaster.ca/~/peace/
www.humanities.mcmaster.ca/gandhi/festival/

In Canada:
www.unac.org/
www.physicians_for_global_survival/
www.canadian peace initiative/

International:
www.unesco.org/cpp/uk/projects/
www.mayorsforpeace.org/
www.internationalcitiesofpeace.org/
www.peacealliance.org/
www.nonviolentpeaceforce.org/
www.ippnw.org/
www.icanw.org/

World Listing of Groups:
https://en.wikipedia.org/wiki/List_of_anti-war_organizations

Made in the USA
Charleston, SC
17 September 2016